# THE FINANCIAL CRISIS OF OUR CITIES

✧

Melvin R. Laird, *Moderator*

✧

Hugh Carey
Jacob Javits
Sidney Jones
Charles Percy

A Round Table held on December 10, 1975
and sponsored by
the American Enterprise Institute for Public Policy Research
Washington, D.C.

THIS PAMPHLET CONTAINS THE PROCEEDINGS OF
ONE OF A SERIES OF AEI ROUND TABLE DISCUSSIONS.
THE ROUND TABLE OFFERS A MEDIUM FOR
INFORMAL EXCHANGES OF IDEAS ON CURRENT POLICY PROBLEMS
OF NATIONAL AND INTERNATIONAL IMPORT.
AS PART OF AEI'S PROGRAM OF PROVIDING OPPORTUNITIES
FOR THE PRESENTATION OF COMPETING VIEWS,
IT SERVES TO ENHANCE THE PROSPECT
THAT DECISIONS WITHIN OUR DEMOCRACY WILL BE BASED
ON A MORE INFORMED PUBLIC OPINION.
AEI ROUND TABLES ARE ALSO AVAILABLE ON
AUDIO AND COLOR-VIDEO CASSETTES.

ISBN 0-8447-2077-1
LIBRARY OF CONGRESS CATALOG CARD NO. 76-3227

*PRINTED IN UNITED STATES OF AMERICA*

**M**ELVIN LAIRD, moderator of the Round Table: Welcome to another public policy forum sponsored by the American Enterprise Institute. Our subject today is the financial crisis of our cities. On the panel we have Assistant Secretary of the Treasury for Economic Policy Sidney Jones; Senator Charles Percy, the senior U.S. senator from the state of Illinois, who of course, has a very close relationship with one of the major cities of the United States, Chicago; Senator Jacob Javits, the senior U.S. senator from the state of New York (you will recall that New York and especially New York City have recently had some serious problems), and Governor Hugh Carey of New York, who will be joining us in a few moments; he has been delayed in transit from National Airport.

The questions we anticipate discussing today are these: Whether the problems of New York are symptomatic of the problems of other cities in the United States; whether the financial crisis that faces the cities is the result of a white-collar population shift; whether the problems of the cities have to do with their age and with a shift in business location that is natural over time; whether the cities can survive in this particular decade; and whether they can perform the necessary services for their citizens. To begin, I would like to ask Sidney Jones if the Department of the Treasury believes that the problems of New York are symptomatic of the problems facing other cities.

SIDNEY JONES, assistant secretary of the treasury for economic policy: I think the answer is both Yes and No.

1

Every city faces the problems of recession and inflation, a combination that erodes the tax base and makes the provision of services much more expensive. To that extent the answer is Yes. However, many cities and states were moving toward surplus by 1972-1973 before the recession caught them, but New York City was not. While New York City, with its particularly difficult problems, may show what would happen to all cities and states when their financial problems reach an advanced stage, most cities and most states have not advanced to that stage. To that extent the answer is No.

MR. LAIRD: Senator Javits, can New York City change so that in the future it can live within its receipts and have a balanced financial picture?

JACOB JAVITS, United States senator (Republican, New York): My answer is Yes—it can and it will. The federal government, through the intercession of the Congress and President Ford, has enabled New York, for the next three years, to deal with the seasonal cash problem every business and every city has—that the receipts come in after the expenditures in any given year. In New York, that delay in cash flow may be as great as $2.3 billion a year. The United States will lose nothing by guaranteeing $2.3 billion: the loan is fully secured and made on a revolving basis for one year. Nevertheless, the loan will enable the city to make it through the next three years—years of privation and sacrifice and a sharp diminution of services.

The city's adjustment will depend on the following questions. First, will the discipline of the citizens be such that they will make up for the diminution of services by their own self-help and voluntary activities? I believe it will. Second, will the business community, at the end of the three years, have enough confidence in New York to put the investment in brains and money into New York that are necessary for it to continue as our premier city? If not, New York will go rapidly downhill. The city will not be able to raise funds in the public markets much before five years are up, and perhaps seven, or even ten.

The nation and the state must become more enlightened in the treatment of their cities. The cities essentially have revolutionary war political borders with no relation whatever to present social and economic conditions or the demography of this country. The business community must invest its resources in bringing the cities up to date, as I believe the federal government will, and the states will. If that happens, New York will have a promising future. If on the other hand our hopes for this investment are dashed, New York will share a common fate with other old cities and go rapidly downhill.

MR. LAIRD: Senator Percy has a constituency in the city of Chicago. Now we do not hear so much about Chicago's problems as we do about New York's. Does Chicago have any problems?

CHARLES PERCY, United States senator (Republican, Illinois): Of course Chicago has problems. Chicago is the second largest metropolitan area in the country, and it has some of the same problems that New York and every other urban area have faced. Since World War II, there has been a shift of business—which has grown rapidly outside the city and declined in the city—and of the affluent white population—which has gone to the suburbs, taking the tax base with it. The federal government has accelerated that shift by building superhighways and expressways (making easy commutation possible both in the suburbs and between the suburbs and the city), and by the subsidization of middle-income Americans through the Federal Housing Administration (making it possible for them to build and own their own homes in the suburbs).

Chicago has also been hurt—every city has—by a high crime rate, by inflation, and by severe restrictions on the states. In Illinois, this restriction has recently caused the state to deny assistance to Chicago's schools. Chicago has the same problems as New York, but what we have that New York does not is a stable government. For twenty years we have had a mayor who knows every in and out of the city and who is a sound fiscal conservative. Because of his fiscal conservatism, he has been backed by many Republican businessmen. And he has run a very tight ship.

3

He has had deep and close cooperation from the industrialists and the banking community in running that tight ship, and of course, he has absolute control over his city council. Mayor Daley is the big difference between Chicago with its double A bond rating and New York with its federal assistance.

MR. LAIRD: Can New York bring in fiscal discipline during the next three to four years?

SENATOR JAVITS: I believe it can. I think that the vale of tears through which the city is passing must be a sobering and constructive experience. There is a solid base in New York and the city's troubles can be overcome, even with the usual "10 percent" for corruption, waste, gold plating, politics, and so on—even call it "15 percent" (and I have heard no estimate that places the fraud and the chicanery in New York above 15 percent).

Now, I think Senator Percy is absolutely right. Whether Chicago is sitting on a keg of dynamite because so much has been covered up and sat on for so many years, only time will tell, but in the meantime we can say Chicago has done very much better than New York. And now, because our hearts have been much bigger than our pocketbooks in New York, we have to cut our cloth accordingly. I do not believe this should occasion any diminution of the basic services in New York because it is in the basic services that the citizens' own self-help comes in. Nevertheless, we have to build up our self-help in the next few years, and there will have to be concentration on business and financial matters by elected officials.

New York has suffered from demographic change. We have taken from the South and the civil rights revolution probably as many as a million and a half people who left the South because of inhospitable conditions there, and we have taken almost a million from Puerto Rico because Puerto Ricans are Americans and are free to travel where they want within our country. Of course, if our country wanted to restrain travel and violate the Constitution or change it, New York could do much better. But, as it is, the people come to New York, as my parents came to New

York from Central Europe—and I am sure my parents' manners may not have been much better than those of some of the present newcomers to New York. I believe these new New Yorkers will change too, but we do need a transition period to work out the city's destiny. I think we will make it, but I think I must give an account here of what has caused our difficulties and what justifies the intercession of the federal government. It is hardly fair to blame it on New York that we pay a living welfare tab— roughly $80 per person per month—while in another state like Mississippi, the payment is somewhere between $20 and $30, and the people cannot live on it. They move, and where they move to is where their relatives are—New York.

MR. LAIRD: Of course New York City only bears about 20 percent of that welfare cost itself. The state and the federal government pick up the rest of that bill.

SENATOR JAVITS: Yes, New York City picks up 25 percent, but then Chicago picks up none, and there are few states that require their cities to pick up any part of the welfare load. That 25 percent is a neat $600 million a year. Now, New York has taken every rap in the book, because it was thought by its own people—not to mention the people of the rest of the country—that New York's wealth was limitless. "New York can take it," they would say, "all the banks, all the brokerage firms, all the airlines, all the radio networks, everything, New York's got it all." But New York did not have it all: there was no bottomless source of money. And today we are facing painful reality.

MR. LAIRD: The Department of the Treasury changed its position after New York City and New York State met the requirements that had been set forth by Secretary of the Treasury Simon, and concurred in by the President. New York City and New York State did meet these particular conditions. The Congress has acted. What is the present risk to the federal government, now that the Senate and House of Representatives have passed the bill and the President has signed it?

MR. JONES: From the very beginning, Secretary Simon was miscast as the villain. He was cast as being heartless or unconcerned, but I have seen how many hours he put into this and nothing could have been further from the truth than the notion that he did not care. He had six points in mind. First of all, and this was the real sacrifice, he wanted the city's budget to be balanced. To balance that budget will not be easy, because it will take cuts of $200 million this year, $270 million next year, and $270 million the next year, with no cost increases (say from inflation) in the interim. There is a significant risk that these cuts cannot be made or that costs will rise from inflation. Second, from the very beginning, he had to consider the problem, "If New York City, what about other cities, or even states?" If we guaranteed New York's bonds, can we stop there? This raises the issues of federal, state, and city political relationships—the power and authority of those who are elected at the local level and the state level. The third point was that New York City would have to restructure its debt. If one teaches finance, which I did, he learns that there are certain fundamental things to be done in this restructuring—scaling down interest charges, delaying the payments of interest or principal, cutting expenditures, and even raising taxes. The fourth point—and while the secretary has mentioned this frequently, it still has not received much attention—is a reconsideration of the formula for federal revenue sharing. About 70 percent of the U.S. population lives in 265 metropolitan centers, and about 70 percent of the federal grants—which will total over $56 billion this year—is given to those 265 metropolitan centers. So there is comparability between grants and population, but no one really knows whether we are allocating the funds properly. Fifth, the secretary wanted to look at the municipal bond market, to see if there were some reforms needed there. And sixth, he wanted the question to be considered whether we need a national standard for city accounting? If cities and states are going to sell their bonds in a national market, are they all going to be subject to uniform accounting rules, uniform disclosure rules, uniform standards of propriety?

MR. LAIRD: Senator Percy, as you look at New York City's debt and New York State's debt and compare the city and state with some of the other areas in the United States, do you believe reforms are needed in municipal financing? Do you believe we might revise the tax-exempt status of municipal bonds and perhaps substitute non-exempt federally insured bonds?

SENATOR PERCY: I think reforms are needed. I think, as Secretary Simon suggested, that we need more accountability and better accounting in the cities. A city can issue bonds in circumstances where corporate executives would be thrown in jail if they issued bonds. Not only do the cities give the bond purchaser virtually no information, they mislead the bond purchaser in what they do give. Elmer Staats, the comptroller general of the United States, told the U.S. Senate just this week that there would be no use in auditing the District of Columbia's books because the books are in such horrible shape that an auditor could not even make sense of them. Now, if a corporation's books were in that shape, the SEC would file against the corporation. We have had regulated corporate bonds and corporate financial structuring for years, and I think we need to have the same thing for our cities if we are to put them on a sound fiscal basis.

Senator Javits has raised the issue whether Chicago is sitting on a keg of dynamite. We do not want to say unjust things that would destroy the rating of our cities. Not every city in this country is in bad shape—in fact many of them are in good shape. Chicago, for example, is in much better shape than the state of Illinois, while in New York the situation is reversed and the state is in better shape than the city. Senator Javits, in pushing for federal aid to New York City, has done a magnificent job against the worst odds I have ever seen, an uphill battle every step of the way. But in Chicago, we have tried to do things in another way: never to spend more than we have taken in. Even in tax anticipation notes, in short-term borrowing, which New York uses far too heavily, we have never borrowed more than 75 percent of our tax receipts. New York has gone right up to 100 percent—

SENATOR JAVITS: And more.

SENATOR PERCY: —and sometimes more, because the city has misled the purchasers of the anticipation notes as to what the revenues were going to be. New York overstates its revenues, while Chicago understates its revenues. Today, New York has a $1,678 per capita indebtedness and Chicago has a $432 per capita indebtedness. In New York the indebtedness went up 102 percent in the last two years while in Chicago it went up 62 percent. Even with inflation Chicago is holding the lid down. And debt as a percentage of property evaluation is 16 percent in New York, and only 4 percent in Chicago: Chicago is not sitting on a keg of dynamite. Chicago is a soundly structured city in very good shape, indeed in better shape than the state of Illinois. The ratio of indebtedness to income is 9 percent in Chicago and 35 percent in New York. There is really no basis of comparison between the problems of New York and those of Chicago, but as a result of this work that Governor Carey and Senator Javits have carried out, New York is on the road to recovery. I think New York will make it, but to make it will require a tough cooperative effort.

MR. LAIRD: The Joint Economic Committee has been studying the method of distribution of revenue sharing and its effect on this problem. Is the committee ready to recommend some changes?

SENATOR JAVITS: The Joint Economic Committee, of which I am a senior member and Senator Percy is a member, has been studying the question. By the way, I would like to thank Senator Percy for his extraordinary understanding of New York's problems and the help he has been to me and to the city, notwithstanding the fact that it may not have made him very popular in Chicago, Illinois.

MR. LAIRD: Helping New York has not been popular anywhere in the United States. I was out in Arizona the other day and my friend, the Minority Leader of the House of Representatives [John Rhodes], was referred to as "the

Congressman from New York" in a question from the newsmen. I tried to point out that as minority leader he has certain responsibilities to the entire country and that New York's problem was one we all had to understand.

SENATOR JAVITS: I think that one day soon the other cities—and every state has them, including Arizona, with Phoenix and Tucson—will realize that as goes New York, there but for the grace of God go I, and will draw a lesson from it. What I meant when I talked about a keg of dynamite in Chicago was not that I was questioning the soundness of its finance and the fine example it has provided, but that I worry whether basic needs have been suppressed in the interest of keeping a tidy financial situation. To revert to what the Joint Economic Committee is doing, I can say we are indeed studying revenue sharing. I do not believe we ought to propose changing very much in revenue sharing because if we do, we will not get any of the changes we want. But the federal government ought to have more to say about what is done with the revenue that is shared. To many municipalities and many states, revenue sharing is just an extra perquisite and they do not include it in an intelligent way in their budgeting.

MR. LAIRD: We want to welcome the governor of New York, who has made it from the airport. We are glad to have him here. As he knows, we have been discussing the problems of the cities and I should tell him that we have reached the question of possible changes in revenue sharing. It has been pointed out that 70 percent of all federal aid is going to the 70 percent of our people that are in the major metropolitan areas, but that we do not know whether the current distribution formulas are correct.

SENATOR JAVITS: I would like to finish the answer to that. I think the distribution formulas are not fair to the cities. New York City, for example, gets about $250 million a year out of roughly $6 billion in revenue sharing, and even New York State gets only about 10 percent of the total—that is, about $600 million a year. Revenue sharing is not adjusted to need and the concentration of need. It is mainly carried out on the basis of population and the formula may give as much to cities that do not need it as to cities that need it very urgently indeed. If I had any real belief that we would not jeopardize revenue sharing generally by pressing for major reforms, I would press for them. But I believe that we are better off going along with the present situation for a while than pressing for major reforms, because I believe that if we start to change the formula, it is likely to be changed against us—that is, against the big, congested, really needy cities like New York.

SENATOR PERCY: This is really a problem in the way the Senate is constituted, and we face it on almost every issue. With two votes from a state with half a million people and two votes from a state of 20 million people, we have to compromise. In this lies the contrast—and frequently the battle—between the House of Representatives and the Senate, the House organized by population and the Senate by states. Those of us in the Senate from the urban industrial areas fight for the formula that sends the revenue where the people are, and the senators from the smaller states say, "We have the same votes you have. We want our share. In fact, we want a disproportionate share. We want the share based on territory, rather than people."

SENATOR JAVITS: Right. But in the end we may get agreement because members of Congress will begin to realize that what they do not pay in the peas, they will pay in the bananas. In other words, if the cities get in real trouble, the Congress will have to do something about it anyhow, and the members of Congress might as well put the revenue-sharing formula on a basis that will permit revenue sharing to support self-help where self-help is really needed.

MR. LAIRD: Governor Carey, will New York make it?

HUGH CAREY, governor of New York: Of course New York will make it, because the timely help the President recommended is now a certainty. I believe the appropriation will come in time, but the key thing is that we now have the financial basis to rescue the city from default. Nevertheless, "making it" means more than merely avoiding current default. It means the redesign and redirection of federal grant programs to cope with the extension of the population into the suburbs, and it means treating the problems of transportation, housing, and economic development on a regional basis. Houston, for example, is a healthy city because, under the laws of the state of Texas, Houston can follow its sprawling population into the suburbs by annexation and therefore will never lose its tax base. But New York City can watch industry and families move out and watch the families return as commuters for employment or recreation or cultural diversion, while it cannot claim a share of the revenues it needs in the city, because it is difficult or impossible to get a commuter tax or a commuter assessment of any kind through a state legislature. The legislators will not vote for levies that adversely affect the incomes of their constituents who live outside the city that needs the money.

I was on the Ways and Means Committee when we designed the revenue-sharing formula. It is not always the fault of the federal government that a formula is not perfect or workable. We tried to design the formula to fit each of the states, but every time we ran the computer runs on the state of New York, the circuit breakers and the fuses blew on the computer, and the lights popped because, away back, the Duke of York, who was the principal owner of the grants that became New York, gave out feudal estates to his friends; and in villages, towns, counties, and all sorts of government units there is no correspondence between size and organization. In parts of New York there can be a village that is larger than a city, and a county that gets an allotment, while within the county, a city may bear a disproportionate share of the burden. When we tried to fit the formula to a map where the localities differ by name and have different functions by design, we found that the formula did not work.

The federal government has an opportunity, in designing formulas for revenue sharing or any kind of block grant, to require some kind of standardization of bound-

aries and function such as the standardization Connecticut has carried out. The state of Connecticut has the
county unit, by which the courts are organized, and then
within the counties, government is carried on in the towns.
It is much simpler to deal with uniform governmental
entities—counties and towns, with no large cities—than it
is to deal with incorporated villages, unincorporated villages, counties with supervisors, counties with county
legislatures, large towns, small cities, and so on. It is impossible to design a formula where there is no uniform
base for governmental activity within the state. Both within
the state and among states, we should use federal leverage
to support regionalization, without which we will not ever
settle the transportation problems of New York, New Jersey
and Connecticut. In the New York area, economic development is likewise better treated on a tri-state or interstate
basis. The Port of New York Authority, for example, which
goes back to the days of Alfred E. Smith, is a compact
between the states, and is therefore treated as a separate
entity.

Regionalization could pull together the basic strengths
of the region in a better fashion than they are pulled together now, and the federal government would be in a
better position than it is now for designing programs to
treat the entire region.

SENATOR PERCY: But it is my impression that regionalization is one of the things that the people fear. I can see
where regional government does make sense: Cook County,
for example, picks up much of Chicago's health costs,
whereas New York City has to pay those costs itself. But
once there is federal money coming in, we begin to get
federal control, and we begin to get standardization. That
is where our federal system of government might possibly
break down, and the prospect raises fear in the people.
We get the cry to "save our cities" and "save our suburbs"
—all because of the fear that the cities and suburbs will be
standardized. Once the localities start accepting large federal grants, there is bound to be some federal control.

GOVERNOR CAREY: When New York City got in trouble,

the President, Chairman of the Federal Reserve Board Burns, Secretary Simon, and all the others involved, including the Senate Banking Committee and the House Banking Committee, required the city to undertake certain reforms to qualify for federal aid. Those reforms were timely and they were necessary. We were going to do them anyway.

MR. LAIRD: Would you have done them anyway if the game had not become so rough down here in Washington, in the Congress and the executive branch?

GOVERNOR CAREY: We would have done them, but not so quickly as we had to when default was looming on the horizon and, to his credit, the President was requiring these reforms. We were going to get them done anyway, but it took some heavy hauling to do them.

SENATOR PERCY: Did the pressure from Washington also help you in trying to overcome some of the pressure of the labor unions? I am all for labor unions, but when, as in New York, they really—

GOVERNOR CAREY: You did not have a political origin, senator. You came out of Bell and Howell, and you have that belief in private enterprise that is a great thing to have.

SENATOR PERCY: We have labor unions that Mayor Daley deals with in Chicago, and they do not seem to rip off the city the way those in New York seem to have done.

GOVERNOR CAREY: I thought you might bring up Mayor Daley. When he got a Democratic governor, he took many of the functions of the city and gave them to the state: welfare, housing, courts, all of those things. He put them under the state and got the state to pay for them, so that Mayor Daley can carry on with the job of running police, fire and sanitation. He can do those things well, and be a good mayor.

13

SENATOR PERCY: We had a Republican governor for four years. Indeed, Governor Ogilvie was being lauded by Mayor Daley the other day.

GOVERNOR CAREY: He is being lauded now that Governor Walker is governor. In any case, what Mayor Daley did was to take functions he believed the city could no longer handle with its tax base and transfer them to the state, and he could do this because he had an accommodation with the Democratic governor. Mayor Beame would like to do the same thing with me, and I well may inherit the jail, the corrections, the courts, and some of the City University of New York problems on a plan and program basis. I suspect that inheritance is inevitable. The states, with their broader tax base, and working with the federal government, will have to take on functions that have historically been handled by cities. The cities can no longer manage to run a transportation system, a university system, a hospital and health system, a pier and wharf system. All these things that normally would be handled by a state have been handled by New York City with a narrowing tax base.

MR. LAIRD: Are you finding out those were great years in the House of Representatives?

GOVERNOR CAREY: Yes. They were. I was able to point a leveled finger of criticism constantly at the mismanagement of state and local government as I became part of it.

SENATOR JAVITS: There is one important thing we have to remember from the civil rights struggles. States' rights were a big issue then, and the argument we made, we who were for the civil rights legislation, was that states' rights are fine so long as you have a performance standard. If the states will do the job, that is fine, but if they will not do the job, then the United States has to step in to do it. I think this is the issue that Senator Percy and Governor Carey have posed. If the states will really do the job and do it effectively, then I think the sentiment in Washington is very strong that the responsibility should devolve downward. But if the states, as they showed in the civil rights struggle, are unable to do the job, or unwilling to do it, then the federal government must. Even with the disadvantages cited by Senator Percy, it remains true that the people expect our country to be run right, and if the federal government has to step in to run it right, the people will want it to step in. That is what the federal government is there for.

Nevertheless, we must give every opportunity to the states and localities to do the job for themselves first: that, it seems to me, is the whole principle of federalism. The principle broke down in civil rights, and it has not been working very well so far in this field of local and state government, but we want it to work. And if we can do better because of New York's great trouble, which is a lesson to the country, I will personally be delighted and, as a senator, I will aid in every way I can. But I will not see basic functions essential to the people go unperformed merely because I do not want to see the federal government carrying out what is the states' responsibility.

GOVERNOR CAREY: I concur with the senator on this. The idea of the block grant is to get away from the bureaucracy and the categorical programs that lay down a high number of specific requirements. The block grant works very well. Revenue sharing was recognized and rated by Richard Nathan of the Brookings Institution as 95 percent effective in its implementation, because the formula works simply: the secretary of the treasury simply requires an audit and report and requires (which is a good thing) that the uses of the money must be advertised before the money is used, so that the public will know what the money is being used for. The money is not to be used for geraniums planted around the town parking lot and so forth, but (perhaps) for a better communication system for the police department. The idea of a block grant with a simple control on it has a great appeal because we now have, at county levels, legislators and executives who can allocate the money effectively without constant federal bureaucratic direction and control.

Where can we use block grants? We can use block grants to better effect in housing. We had the old Section 236 program; now we have Section 8, which is not working. With as many stipulations as it has, Section 8 does not always fit the demographic or geopolitical problems of a given area or region. We can use block grants in mass transit, because different areas need different kinds of transportation systems—bus or monorail or combinations of rail and bus—and the states are equipped to design these and have them function. The block grant system can also work in economic development. The more we move to block grants, the more we will get rid of some of the overload of bureaucracy at the federal level—which will be a saving—and the more effective will be the performance of the objectives of the federal government in housing, transportation, and education. I firmly believe that the block grant will give us maximum initiative in attacking our local and state problems.

SENATOR PERCY: I would like to suggest a solution, at least for discussion—a solution that involves the executive branch of government as well as our votes in the Congress. I think the Highway Trust Fund has to be dissolved: right now it is a disaster. It has an $8.5 billion surplus of unspent money, while we have completed over 99 percent of the national highway system. That money sits there, and it leads the states to pave over everything while mass transit systems are starving. So, let us dissolve it—let us create a national transportation trust fund, or else put the Highway Trust Fund money in general revenue and see if we can have a sensible, integrated transportation system and not merely a system based on building more of the highways that are causing our problems. Highways lead us to get out of the city all the more, to move farther out —to move the affluent out—to move the factories out. They let the workers commute by automobile, which is certainly making us far more beholden to Arab oil, to the OPEC countries, than we should be. It would be in the national interest to get rid of this dependence on highways, but how do we do it?

MR. LAIRD: Would Mr. Jones like to comment on that?

MR. JONES: Yes, I would like to. The appropriations may be there, but I can assure you the money is not there. The Treasury runs about a $3- to $6-billion cash balance, and there is no big bag of money marked "Highway Trust Fund."

SENATOR PERCY: Which is why people worry about social security, too.

MR. LAIRD: In this discussion, it seems everyone is saying that the federal government—whether by block grants or revenue sharing or what—will be footing the bills. We are going to have a federal deficit this year of some $80 billion, and President Ford is struggling to submit a fiscal 1977 budget that will hold the deficit to $40 billion. Where is this money for these programs going to come from?

MR. JONES: I am impressed with any discussion that emphasizes state and local responsibility because there is a tendency to say all would be well if only the federal government would do these things. First of all, federal grants and loan programs have in fact increased. They were $7 billion in 1960, and are about $60 billion this year. That represents a 14 percent annual rate of growth. The transfer payments are up to about $180 billion this year. We are carrying out redistribution. But there is a fundamental point of economics we have tended to ignore, and that is that we cannot consume more than we produce. The federal government has run a deficit in fourteen out of the last fifteen years. The federal budget was $134 billion in 1966. This year, it will be over $370 billion. In the decade from 1966 through 1975, the cumulative federal deficit was $145 billion, and in the off-budget programs the net borrowings (not the loan exposure) were another $150 billion. If the loans ever go sour, we will be getting into the kind of discussion we have had over social security —but that is another story. In any case, the federal government has taken a third of a trillion dollars out of the capital markets during a single decade. And that is only the prologue. This year we will run a deficit of over $70 billion. And, if all goes well, which it rarely does, we will still run up a $40 or $50 billion deficit next fiscal year.

SENATOR PERCY: That is why we have to cut out some programs, or cut the trust fund out. Or is there somewhere else we can make the cuts?

MR. JONES: Cutting programs is not the answer to the whole problem, but—

SENATOR PERCY: We were paying farmers for not producing crops: we saved $4 to $5 billion there. Now, we can afford to feed people that are malnourished. But we could not do both: we had to do one or the other.

MR. JONES: Our problem is that when we try to identify a specific program to eliminate, we run into difficulties with the beneficiaries, with the congressional oversight committee, and with the executive office agency that is running the program.

SENATOR PERCY: Senator Javits and I took care of Secretary Laird's ABM. We saved—how much did we save? You know what I mean—that technological pile of junk the secretary was trying to shove down our throats over there.

MR. LAIRD: We saved $120 billion by the ABM treaty. It was a very important thing to have that treaty negotiated.

SENATOR PERCY: Right. You can feed a lot of people with that money.

MR. LAIRD: If we had not been able to get the treaty, we would have spent $120 billion. The only reason we got the treaty is that the majority of the Senate did not take Senator Percy's position.

GOVERNOR CAREY: Let a converted, liberal, moderate, fiscal conservative get in here for a minute and talk to this. This question of off-balance-sheet funding and borrowing is a key matter the federal government must address. New

York got into great difficulty, and the whole country is in great difficulty, through off-balance-sheet funding and lending. The lead organization for social purpose housing and the Urban Development Corporation almost went into default because no one had oversight responsibility. We had a good idea, but it was mismanaged. Nevertheless, we saved it. But the off-balance-sheet activities of the federal government and of the state and local governments need more oversight and regulation. I would suggest that, if we are going to use the Highway Trust Fund differently, we should use it for seed money to create liquidity, and let it be a multiplier, with a guarantee mechanism and regulation of lending. Now, the federal government has guarantee mechanisms on the books, but Mr. Lynn in the Office of Management and Budget does not care for them, so the guarantee mechanism for housing is not being implemented.

Let us give the states guarantees that do not affect the federal government—regulate the way that the states can use those guarantees so that they can build and provide jobs—and then we can get the multiplier effect of federal dollars without actual expenditure. We will create a better form of liquidity, and the states can cure their own problems if we give them the guarantees.

MR. JONES: Let me emphasize the fact that, if we do put in seed money or any kind of money, we will have to raise the money, because there is none.

GOVERNOR CAREY: The money will have to be raised only if the states default on the guarantees.

MR. JONES: I understand. But we would still have to get the original money if we were going to transfer funds. There is no bag of money sitting somewhere that can be diverted to new programs.

GOVERNOR CAREY: I think Mr. Jones is ignoring the successful effect of the Federal Deposit Insurance Corporation or of the Federal Housing Administration. Those are money-makers for the federal government and yet they get housing built and they insure depositors against losses. Let us look at the record of the guarantee mechanisms in federal government at the Export-Import Bank. Let us use that guarantee system so we can use the credit resources of the federal government, regulate the uses of the money borrowed, and make certain that the revenue streams are there to pay off the obligations. We will then get housing built and we will then get highways and transportation built. We will get it done because of the multiplier effect of the investment capital that will come forward from the private sector, and we will be able to carry out local borrowings if the regulation is there to guarantee that the revenue stream is adequate to retire the capital investment.

MR. JONES: Of course. I agree with guarantees for a few specific programs. All I was saying was that the original money—

GOVERNOR CAREY: Unfortunately, your boss does not, and that is the problem.

MR. JONES: —the original money is what you have to get from somewhere. This year, the—

GOVERNOR CAREY: Senator Percy mentioned the Highway Trust Fund, which is $8 billion.

MR. JONES: I tell you, there is no money there, only an appropriation.

GOVERNOR CAREY: If that is an appropriation it is a pretty big one.

SENATOR PERCY: No, no. There is a tag on the money—

MR. JONES: There may be a tag, but there is no money.

SENATOR PERCY: There is a "first call" on it. By law, the money must be spent for the specified purposes of the act.

MR. JONES: We have weekends when we almost run out. And, this year, we will have to go—

MR. LAIRD: I think it should be clear there is no cash balance in the Highway Trust Fund. There is no cash balance in the social security fund.

MR. JONES: That is the point I was trying to make.

MR. LAIRD: If we are going to spend those moneys, we will have to borrow to spend them, because there is no cash balance.

MR. JONES: Or else we will have to divert the revenues from somewhere else.

SENATOR JAVITS: Yes, but the important thing here is that we have all said what can be done on the negative: cut expenses, cut the deficit, hold things down. America has never grown that way, though we will do it because we have to.

MR. JONES: No, no. I never said anything about cutting the federal budget. All we want to do is slow down the momentum of it. The budget has gone up 38 percent in two years—

GOVERNOR CAREY: Wait a minute. Wait a minute. When we slow down the momentum, we are putting my people out of work. We have 12 percent unemployment in New York. I would like this panel to look at the history of the Reconstruction Finance Corporation, under Franklin Delano Roosevelt. The RFC was begun under Herbert Hoover, but Franklin Roosevelt put it to work, and Jesse Jones ran it. It made money for the federal government, while it took plants and even localities that were collapsing, and brought them back to life and supplied jobs. And it was a guarantee mechanism: it provided that, if this plant were built, or this business continued to operate, the government would put the capital behind the business, in the form of a guarantee to get the plant into production or keep the business operating. When liquidity had developed again and capital was being returned through profits, the government would be paid back. It worked. It would work again.

MR. LAIRD: We are getting away from the subject here, the financial crisis of our cities.

GOVERNOR CAREY: The financial crisis of the city of New York will never be solved as long as we have 12 percent unemployment across the state and 20 percent unemployment in the ghettos and 37 percent unemployment among young minority men and women in the cities, who are out of school and out of work.

SENATOR JAVITS: There is no question about that. New York's deepest endemic problem is the fact that we do not really try to implement the Full Employment Act of 1946. To implement the act will take investment and enterprise. It will not be done by the dead hand of restriction. That is what the governor is saying, and I thoroughly agree with him.

MR. LAIRD: Just in passing, I would like to note that as one travels around this country—and I have recently been in Arizona and Illinois, Wisconsin and Minnesota—there is no understanding of that problem, and there is strong criticism of what are viewed as high living, high pensions, high salaries, in New York City. I do not think New York's story has gotten across very well. And for it to get across, there is going to have to be some discipline in the cities, too.

SENATOR JAVITS: I could not agree with you more about the discipline, but we must also keep our eye on the fact that positive measures have always been America's salvation—that we must add to America's stock of wealth.

MR. JONES: As you know, our basic thrust in the Department of the Treasury has been to increase capital investment. But it is difficult to increase capital investment when the federal budget rises 38 percent in two years, and when the federal government comes in and takes a third of a trillion dollars out of the money and capital markets in ten years. We are trying to slow down this eerie momentum that has really eroded our fiscal ability.

**M**R. LAIRD: It is time now to turn to the second portion of our program on the financial crisis of our cities. This portion includes audience participation, and we have a great many people in our audience who may wish to ask questions of the panel. Who in our audience will be the first?

JAMES GELBRICK, staff, House Banking Committee: I should say I am speaking for myself in this question, which I would like to direct to Assistant Secretary Jones. The current plan to rescue New York City, the terms of which were imposed largely by the President, rests on three very tenuous props: (1) a moratorium on the repayment of city notes, which was imposed by the state legislature, and which may be found unconstitutional by the courts; (2) a $2.5 billion investment of pension fund money, which may be found to be in violation of the "prudent man" rule for fiduciary investments; and (3) a program of short-term loans from the U.S. Treasury, which can only be issued if the secretary is virtually certain they will be repaid—in other words, if the other two-thirds of the program are sustained. The whole edifice seems to me to resemble a three-legged stool constructed without nails.

My two questions to Mr. Jones are, first, Is this, in his view, a defensible way to approach a potential national disaster? and, second, what will the Treasury do if the house of cards collapses?

MR. JONES: I would disagree with the first comment. New York is a viable city with a large revenue base. New York has increased that revenue base. There has been tangible progress toward making those needed corrections that Senator Javits and Governor Carey identified. With the program that has been developed and presented in good faith by the state and by the city, the secretary of the treasury will move ahead. I do not see this as a potential national disaster. In fact, from the very beginning, the issue had to be divided into a financial part and a psychological part. The financial part has been well handled by the financial markets in the traditional manner. The psychological part was uncertain, which is why it was so important to have the state and the city make the tangible progress they have made. Now we take their moves on good faith. And the secretary, I assume, will base his decisions accordingly.

MR. LAIRD: Yes?

RICHARD NATHAN, Brookings Institution: I address my question to the whole panel. At Brookings, we have done some research on the social and economic problems of central cities, and what we found is that the central cities, the core cities, with the deepest problems, are located particularly in the northeastern and north central regions of this nation, while in the West, the Southwest and the South, we found many cases where central cities are much better off than their suburbs—where, with annexation and consolidation, there are no core city problems. Now, that seems to me to point at a question. How can we devise a federal aid strategy that does not, in effect, punish people who have consolidated and expanded and reformed local government in the West and in the South, by aiding the older cities in the northeastern and north central regions that have core city problems and that have not taken the steps to spread burdens and reform government?

My question really sums up to this: How can we devise federal aids that do not discriminate against people who do good things in an effort to aid the core cities with the deepest problems? To me, this is a central dilemma that has been alluded to in various ways, and I would like to hear some direct comments on it, if I could.

MR. LAIRD: Perhaps Senator Javits could comment on that first, and then we will go to Governor Carey and then to Senator Percy.

SENATOR JAVITS: I really do not think it is a dilemma if we remember what our older cities have contributed to

24

this country. The United States owes our older cities a great debt, going way back before we became a country. The fact that the problems of these cities are different from those of newer cities and the fact that the cities have to be modernized and brought along, does not mean that their values should not be preserved. It would take, at a minimum, twenty-five to forty years to replace New York as a revenue source for the federal government. New York City produces over $15 billion a year in tax revenues for the federal government. New York gets back, at the most, including transfer payments, $3.5 billion. That represents almost a $12 billion net income for the federal government. It would take twenty-five to fifty years to get that out of a Houston or a Fort Worth and Dallas or some other central place that might replace New York.

For value like this, the United States must show some special understanding for these older cities like New York, with their older troubles, especially where the demography of the country and the constitution require the cities to assume disproportionate burdens. The people from the South, a million-and-a-half in number, are not flocking to some small town in the South, but to New York City. That is a federal problem, and the situation is no different for the Puerto Ricans. Let us remember that today the newly arrived represent one half of New York City's welfare burden.

MR. LAIRD: I wonder, though, if we are addressing the practical political problem of getting the votes in the House and Senate if modernized government is not in effect. In many areas of the South and particularly in the West, the local units of government that Governor Carey was talking about have been modernized.

SENATOR JAVITS: I think we need to have time for reform; that is the time I want to make. New York must have this time because our problems are deeper and more vested and more built-in than those of other cities. But we do have to get on with the job of reform. And the dire results of our inability to reform so far have enormously accelerated the necessity for reform. I would say, first, that the

United States must help, second, that the United States and the separate states must facilitate the reforming process, and third, that the cities must show the will to carry out reform.

GOVERNOR CAREY: May I suggest that Mr. Nathan's question is tied to what Mr. Gelbrick was saying as it relates to the kinds of aids that we can use. What I see is that there is nothing wrong with a little coercive element in the right direction in a federal program. The coercive element I am talking about is an element that would say, "If you want the money, you're going to have to step forward and change your way of doing things."

Regionalization means some annexation. Let me cite a prime example. Two municipalities up in New York, the city of Mechanicsville and the town of Half Moon, which is a very small unit outside the city of Mechanicsville, have been looking toward annexation to unify the school district and the water district. But every year, Mechanicsville votes for annexation, nine to one, and Half Moon defeats it, and the court upholds the defeat of annexation. If, in order for those two to qualify for a proper kind of assistance, there were a coercive element of better aid, the referendum would carry. That coercion is the kind of thing the federal government should do. What I am referring to, as it affects Mr. Gelbrick's question, is that the guarantee bill, which had very specific reforms in it, was a better bill than the one we received from the White House. I can say that now because the President signed the bill. I would not have said it before because he might have thought we did not want the $2.3 billion. Nevertheless, the House bill and the Senate bill—the Proxmire bill and the Reuss bill—were better designed to implement reforms in the city than the bill the President signed.

If the administration would look at the Congress and the congressional budget system and let the representatives of the people work with the governors to design programs to benefit the older parts of our country, to benefit the decaying cities, we would come up with some pretty good ideas. I think we need the governors to step forward to disagree with the political judgments that adversely affect the economies of the Northeast. For example, the worst thing that could have happened in federal energy policy was for us to put a tariff on imported fuels. That tariff was a political judgment that cost the Northeast hundreds of millions of dollars of consumer and public moneys to buy fuel. It was a bad move by the White House and it should never have been undertaken. In fact, it has been challenged in the courts as an improper and illegal use of the presidential power to impose tariffs.

Among the things we suffer from are three of the worst economic decisions of the recent past—decisions economic in effect but all of them political in nature: the fuel tariff, the wheat deal, and the tax cut that was dropped like a piece of batter on a hot stove and dissipated without having any impact on the economy. If the governors had been asked, "Do you want a tax cut or do you want some help through the multiplier effect of guarantees or loans to cities and states to help in their programs?" they would have said, "Keep the tax cut—hold on to it—and let us have the multiplier for public works, for improvements, for transportation: we'll get more jobs and more revenue and more income than you'll get with that tax cut."

MR. LAIRD: Senator Percy?

SENATOR PERCY: Mr. Nathan's question is a good one. I think that, for the most part, federal programs must be directed toward the problems, and the older cities have a preponderance of the problems. But we cannot ever, with the largesse of federal assistance, create a *dis*incentive for cities to do what is in their long-range best interest. We cannot, for instance, bail out any city that has a practice, such as New York has had, of enabling employees to load their last year of employment with overtime for their retirement benefits. We can take specific cases: a man earning $15,000 a year gets $17,000 a year when he retires because he loads that last year with overtime. We can never reward a city that believes it can go on forever with rent control, which distorts the market, provides arbitrarily low rents, and destroys the incentive to build new rental property that can be taxed. We cannot have a system that will forever be an incentive for any city to believe it will be bailed out from the results of those practices that must be discouraged, not encouraged.

GOVERNOR CAREY: What I am talking about is the characteristic philosophy, the coercive element, that says "If you want the federal money, you have to agree to accept the reforms."

MR. LAIRD: I think Governor Carey makes a very interesting point, even though there is a revenue-sharing program in New York State. I agree there should be incentives, as far as federal programs are concerned, but in Wisconsin we handle the annexation problem he referred to through incentives in state legislation. There is no reason New York cannot do what the governor is talking about without coming to the federal government.

GOVERNOR CAREY: But there is. We have an antiquated constitutional provision that says we cannot have annexation without referendum, with both sides agreeing by two-thirds. Until we can change the constitution—we can only have a constitutional convention once every six years or so, and indeed the last reform constitution recommended by the constitutional convention in New York State was defeated —we will have a very difficult time. But the federal government would not be impeded by the New York state constitution. It could disregard the state constitution and say, "If you want this particular aid, you have to qualify for it." That, in a sense, would get around the constitutional barrier, which is otherwise very difficult to avoid.

MR. JONES: Am I fourth in line?

MR. LAIRD: Yes.

MR. JONES: The question that Mr. Nathan asked, I think, is really the fundamental societal question: one has to decide what is a national function and what is a local and state function. Now, if the care and well-being of the people is a national function, which I think we could assume it is, then perhaps the federalizing of welfare would be a legitimate step. But I do not think this means that the people outside of New York City should be required to pay for pension funds, which are not employee-contributed, or tax-free or tuition-free universities and hospitals. If the people want the local and state services, then logic presupposes they should pay for them. The people of New York City, when they pay their $12 billion in taxes, receive the benefits of a Defense Department, of an agricultural research program that helps grow the food that they eat, of a total $370 billion worth of federal outlays: that is the way our system works. Taxes pay for gross benefits, which show up not in individual income or state revenue sharing, but in a defense posture, in a foreign relations posture, in an agricultural research posture, and so on. The decision on the tax cut came from the belief, philosophical and pragmatic, that the people should have the right to decide how they will spend their incomes, and that the incidence of taxation had gone beyond what people are willing to pay for.

GOVERNOR CAREY: But the Treasury did not have the money: the buying deficit was increased.

MR. JONES: Yes, or else there would not have been a deficit in fourteen out of the last fifteen years. The purpose of the tax cut, as distinct from its underlying motivation, and as distinct from its timing, was short-term economic stabilization.

GOVERNOR CAREY: Did we get it?

MR. JONES: Yes.

GOVERNOR CAREY: Did we get recovery?

MR. JONES: Recovery? We have had real final sales increase 4.5 to 5 percent over the last six months. That is an economic recovery.

GOVERNOR CAREY: We do not seem to have found that recovery in New York yet. I wish you would send it up there.

MR. JONES: Well, New York has—

GOVERNOR CAREY: New York has 12 percent unemployment.

MR. JONES: This is another issue on which one has to ask, "Have you attracted industry or driven industry away, with your state and local taxes?"

GOVERNOR CAREY: As soon as we federalize welfare, as soon as we stop talking about it and do it—not that it is Mr. Jones's department, but when the administration federalizes welfare—New York will not need to come ask for help in all the ways it has had to. Welfare is the second largest item in the city budget, and the biggest drain on the county budgets in New York State. When welfare is federalized, New York will not have to come knocking on the door for local aids.

SENATOR PERCY: Are we still on Mr. Nathan's question?

MR. LAIRD: I think we are. I will go to the next question.

MARION BARRY, chairman, Finance and Revenue Committee, District of Columbia City Council: I would like to try to bring this down to some of the realities I see in the cities. I get the impression that the people say, "If you would just manage what you have better, it would be all right." But the increased costs in city governments and even in state governments come in the aid for mothers with dependent children, in Medicaid, in trying to figure out a way to rebuild housing in a city. It seems to me that this is the point that should be made here. It appears the administration is opposed to pushing forward for 100 percent federal funding of welfare, as well as of health benefits. The other part of the question is with Section 8, which is a colossal flop if we measure by the amount of housing it has built.

30

If we have liberalized welfare rules, which would mean that a person could come into Washington and in thirty days get on the rolls (and we do not always ask them to come) and if there is no more land to be used in the cities, what will the administration do to place the burden where it can be borne, and specifically what will the administration do to move toward 100 percent federal payment for welfare and health? I think that 100 percent payment is important beyond any question of national health insurance.

The other area where I have a question is housing, and this is directed to Senator Percy and to Senator Javits. What is the Congress going to do to make the executive come forward with this kind of program or to impose this kind of program on the cities. I resent it when the people say that the eastern cities are mismanaged. There are problems—no question about that. But I suspect, if we were to look at the governments of the Southwest and the West, we would find that they have some antiquated management problems, too. In any case, these are my general concerns and I would like to listen to the assistant secretary and the senators and to anyone else who wants to pitch in.

MR. LAIRD: Assistant Secretary Jones?

MR. JONES: I think we must start by asking, "What are national priorities?" I would say that, once these are arranged in a certain sequence, we can figure out what kinds of revenues we will need to pay for them. Now, if we want to go to the federalizing of welfare payments, which I have said I believe would be a constructive thing, we must recognize that federal welfare payments will not come out of thin air. Someone will have to pay the tax revenues from which the federal welfare payments will come. We do not have the tax revenues to continue to meet the demands we have been putting on our system. If I say what am I going to do about federalizing welfare, I should be required to say what I am going to cut out—as should every member of Congress and every member of the administration who proposes to start a new program.

MR. BARRY: What about the defense budget? That is the kind of thing I meant.

MR. JONES: I am sorry, I misunderstood. We have cut the defense budget by 40 percent in real terms since 1969, while we have doubled social payments in real terms since 1969. There are some—and Mr. Laird may want to comment as a former secretary of defense—who say we may have cut defense too much. In any case, when we say that we want something more done, we have to identify what is being done that will cease being done. That means we have to look at all the federal programs and the federal grants and loans that have gone from $7 billion in 1960 to $60 billion in 1975.

Now, as far as the guarantee programs are concerned, there is a great myth in our system that somehow a guarantee does not cost anyone anything. Principle number two of economics—principle number one being "there is no such thing as a free lunch"—is that, when we give an advantage to someone, we give a disadvantage to everyone else. Where we give the full faith and credit of the federal government to one borrower, we give a disadvantage to every other borrower: there is a cost to guarantees.

I would support the federalization of welfare payments. I would strongly support the negative income tax as a much more efficient means of providing a minimum threshold status, rather than the 1,009 social delivery programs that we have, which tend to be bureaucratic, inefficient, costly, and unsatisfying both to the recipients and to the taxpayers who bear costs greater than they evidently should. What is the administration going to do about it? In 1970 the administration tried the welfare reform bill. It got to the five-yard line but not over the goal. The liberals said, "You're not giving enough," and the conservatives said, "You shouldn't give anything." The program died aborning. But that process can start again, once the people decide that the present situation is intolerable.

GOVERNOR CAREY: Mr. Chairman, may I say something? When you get to the five-yard line and you are about to punch the ball over, you do not give up. You get the ball again, you change your play, and you go over the goal line. I was in the Congress then, and we made a massive effort: we got that bill through the House twice, and it died in the Senate. Now, when he was inaugurated, President Ford said that one of his major goals was the achievement of a national health insurance program. Where is it? And if we are all for the federalization of welfare now, why is the federalization of welfare not a prime objective of this federal government? Why is there no initiative going on right now for the federalization of welfare payments?

I agree with Mr. Barry that federalization of welfare would help the District of Columbia greatly. It would help the state of New York greatly. And, if that is a national policy, why is the administration not out there fighting to get either national health insurance (which the President said would be one of his first objectives) or the federalization of welfare through the Congress? We are not going to have credibility anywhere in the country if we state our objectives and then fail to try to reach them.

MR. LAIRD: I am afraid Governor Carey may not have a very good reading on the Congress right now, just living around New York. I happen to be for those programs. I introduced them and urged the Nixon administration to come up with them. But I can assure you that this co-equal branch of our government, right at the present time, is not of the mind or the attitude to move in those directions. And I think the President would be wasting a lot of the energies that are needed to get some other things through the Congress. I think things like that may be considered in the next session of the Congress, after the next election.

GOVERNOR CAREY: It was said we would never get a federal aid to education bill. The late Senator Taft introduced the first one in 1944, and we passed federal aid to education in 1965. It took a lot of heavy lifting, but it was done.

MR. LAIRD: I introduced revenue sharing for the first time in 1957, but revenue sharing did not pass for almost twenty years.

SENATOR JAVITS: I think that as long as the chairman is talking about us, we had better talk back.

MR. LAIRD: What is your opinion?

SENATOR JAVITS: My opinion is with the governor, because I do believe—and I am very favorable to President Ford, as is well known—that this is the kind of a battle that can be won only by persistence. I would like to ask Mr. Jones if he sees national health insurance of some kind and federalization of welfare on the banner of the administration. The reason I ask this is that neither health insurance nor welfare federalization is as hot a prospect as it sounds for the cities and states. Right now, the federal government pays a great part of welfare. Even New York City gets 50 percent and so does New York State. Other states, Mississippi, for example, get up to 83 percent. There is argument about the formula, but that is the situation.

Now I think it can be demonstrated that an intelligent plan of national health insurance would reduce the cost of health care to the American people, if we add up Medicaid and Medicare and what the people are paying out of their own pockets, especially considering the way in which in many cases they are overpaying because of the disorganization of this system. So I strongly urge the President, notwithstanding the uphill battle, to put national health insurance high on his list of priorities, to propose measures for it, and to leave it to people like Senator Percy and me to fight hard for them.

In this New York City situation, the President added the final decisive touch: that is the role of an American President. Without that touch, aid to New York City would not have happened—though with it, it would not have happened either, if we had not been able to muster the support of the Congress. The situation is the same in health insurance. If the President would put national health insurance high on his list, give us his idea as to how it should be implemented by proposing a tangible bill, like the New York City bill he sent—and, incidentally, that bill was passed practically the way he sent it—I think we could do something with it. But if we have no feeling that the administration gives national health insurance a high priority or that it is administration policy, we will not get action.

SENATOR PERCY: I would like to answer Mr. Barry by asking him to put himself in our shoes. I think persistence is what is needed, but we are up against something that in this bicentennial year I would call factions in government, using the language of *Federalist* Paper No. 10. For instance, the food surplus program was not designed to feed hungry people, but to take off the hands of the farmers crops they did not want. Those were not necessarily the crops that the people wanted to eat, but that is what started us feeding the hungry. We persisted and we changed the whole idea of that program. We are going to persist on the Highway Trust Fund, which is supported by highway lobbyists who want to make money building roads and automobiles. We are going to break the Highway Trust Fund because its continuation is no longer in the national interest, but breaking it is going to take persistence.

In housing, we are under pressure from the mortgage people, the home builders. They want to keep building new homes in the suburbs. There is no incentive to build them in the city, in an area where the builders must take risks. But overbuilding the suburbs is not in the national interest. As Secretary of Housing and Urban Development Carla Hills will tell you, we could build rehabilitated housing in the city, in the inner city, where it is really needed, for 50 percent less than the cost of new construction in the suburbs, and doing this would build the cities rather than contribute to their decay. But we have to fight these lobbyists. We are fighting them. We will persist and we will win in the long run. But we need help and understanding. As legislators, we try to legislate against these factions, these special interests, which are a part of the fiber of our political system.

MR. LAIRD: Who will be next?

MARCIA KASS, Bureau of National Affairs: I would like to ask Senator Javits what he meant by the citizens having the discipline to take over the essential services, and what his reaction is to Senator Proxmire's report that there were no emergency plans to take over essential services in New York.

SENATOR JAVITS: What I meant was that the citizens could fill in as volunteers—and I will give you practical examples of that—in jobs that would be left open, in services that would not be rendered, with the strict economies in force in the city and required by the state and by the nation. For example, we would have watchers of fire alarm posts so that the 50 percent of the fire departments' time which is taken up with answering false alarms would be cut down materially. We would have auxiliary police who could deal with school crossings and clerical work in the police department, and even take over some of the jobs of what we call meter maids.

By the way, anyone who goes to New York City will see what has happened there—the traffic tangle is worse than ever, the double and triple parking is worse than ever —and until we reshape our organization to deal with the shortages left by these necessary economies (as with containerization of garbage, and the concentration of garbage at one point so that the city pick-up truck has to stop only once and can therefore make fewer calls per week), we will not come out on top.

These things are citizen efforts. Now I thoroughly agree with Senator Proxmire's letter to the cabinet departments. We cannot run a government and assume that there is going to be sunshine every day: we have to be ready to deal with emergency situations, and have a plan on the shelf instead of being in a panic. And we must have training to implement that plan, just as in the civil defense days, which, by the way, represented very intelligent planning, and we may yet rue the day that we threw civil defense into the discard.

MARVIN KOSTERS, American Enterprise Institute: I have heard some discussion here about federal loan guarantees. It is often said that these guarantees do not cost the government a penny. I would like to ask Governor Carey and

Mr. Jones whether these guarantees do cost anyone anything, and, if so, how the process works.

GOVERNOR CAREY: I am glad you asked that question, because the answers show a fundamental difference between my views and those of the administration on how to help in a situation where there is a need for liquidity and capital. For instance, on Monday morning December 15th, unless we find the money, one of the best managed and most effective housing finance agencies in the country will go into default. It should not go into default. The reason it may go into default is that capital markets are closed because of the New York syndrome. I am down in Washington today to seek some kind of a band-aid or a tiding over of that agency to avoid a default.

Thirty other states have similar moral-obligation borrowing agencies. For the federal government to guarantee the paper of that particular agency would not cost a dime: the Lockheed loan made money, and it was a guarantee by the federal government. What Mr. Jones has said—with due regard to the view that guarantees would give advantages to one city and disadvantages to all the others—will not hold water. Guarantees are a successful way, an effective way, of putting the credit behind something that deserves a credit back-up. If an agency or a state or a city does not deserve the credit, we should not give the guarantee. If there is a price to be exacted for the guarantee, then we should exact the price to make money on the guarantee, and not make the borrowing tax-exempt with a guarantee of preferred security.

But as long as there is a closed mind against guarantee, and as long as there is the idea that it is better to loan money and affect the federal government than use the guarantee mechanism, we are not going to get anywhere.

The House Banking Committee under Henry Reuss put forth a program for guarantees for housing in marginal income areas. But Mr. Lynn of the Office of Management and Budget is against it, and the Department of Housing and Urban Development will not use the law that is on the books that would enable us to build more housing than we have built under Section 8, which Marion Barry describes

37

as an utter failure. Why can the guarantee mechanism, which is in FHA, VHA, the Export-Import Bank, and which worked effectively in the Lockheed loan, not be used to help in what is clearly a liquidity problem in the entire United States? Right now—

MR. LAIRD: I want equal time for Mr. Jones on that—

GOVERNOR CAREY: —local and—

MR. LAIRD: You are filibustering. You ought to be in the Senate.

GOVERNOR CAREY: Right now local and state governments across this country have gone $7.9 billion into the red. New York is not the only one in trouble. So, I say, use the guarantee mechanism. It will make some money for the federal government, it will cure the liquidity crisis, and it will really get something moving in this country.

MR. LAIRD: Mr. Jones. Thirty seconds.

MR. JONES: There are limited areas where the loan guarantee programs can help, such as in the SBA and SBIC examples. In housing, we put $22 billion into the mortgage markets in 1974, but I am not sure we added one dollar of mortgage money to those markets. I will let Senator Percy go from that point.

SENATOR PERCY: I have never heard such discussion. I am sorry that a former member of the House Ways and Means Committee would really believe the things Governor Carey is saying. What a change between Washington and Albany. If I went to Governor Carey and I said, "I have a friend who has a very bad debt payment record, who is just on the brink of bankruptcy, but I am going to ask you to guarantee his loan," and he did guarantee that loan, would he have to disclose that to a bank when he wanted to borrow more money for himself? You bet he would. That would be a potential liability. And every time we put the guarantee of the government of the United States behind bonds for New York City or New York State, or the city of Chicago or the state of Illinois, we would have to consider whether they were going to be paid off.

GOVERNOR CAREY: Exactly. We should not give the guarantee unless there was a clear ability for repayment.

SENATOR PERCY: Which means it cannot be said that it does not cost a penny. Potentially, it may cost 100 percent of that loan. Potentially, it may—

GOVERNOR CAREY: No, no senator, I must disagree, because the back-up for the guarantee is this—

SENATOR PERCY: Well, I just asked the good assistant secretary here whether we can put the federal government's signature on a guarantee without any risk incurred—

GOVERNOR CAREY: The back-up for the guarantee is that if the guarantee was not repaid other federal funds would be impounded to discharge the guarantee obligation.

MR. JONES: Well, the fact is that—

GOVERNOR CAREY: You cannot oversimplify this.

MR. JONES: The fact is that the—

MR. LAIRD: That is the cost, you see. That is the cost.

GOVERNOR CAREY: Yes, but the federal government does not lose the money.

MR. LAIRD: There is a cost involved. I think this is important, and I would like to hear from Mr. Jones on this.

GOVERNOR CAREY: Mr. Jones said it works for the SBA, it works for the SBIC, then why will it not work here?

MR. JONES: But the idea that it does not cost anything is wrong. When you have a borrower who gets the full faith and credit of the government, he borrows at a lower rate than he would otherwise—which means that others will have to borrow at higher rates. That is the cost.

GOVERNOR CAREY: The Treasury Department charges a premium in order to equalize that, and then makes the money.

MR. JONES: We do?

GOVERNOR CAREY: The Treasury charges a premium.

MR. JONES: We do not.

GOVERNOR CAREY: You did.

MR. JONES: Is the governor saying we should? I might agree with that. But if he says we do, I would disagree.

GOVERNOR CAREY: The Treasury had better get together with President Ford, because he is charging us a premium on the $2.3 billion loan to New York City.

MR. JONES: It is to be hoped this is a one-city aberration, not a governmental program.

GOVERNOR CAREY: If that means it was not a good idea to help New York, Mr. Jones had better convince President Ford of that.

SENATOR JAVITS: The fact is, is it not, that the Treasury makes money. The United States has made money consistently on its guarantee program.

SENATOR PERCY: On a no-overhead basis?

SENATOR JAVITS: That is right.

SENATOR PERCY: As Senator Javits knows, the student loan guarantee program alone is a billion dollars in default.

SENATOR JAVITS: But I said—

SENATOR PERCY: A billion dollars.

SENATOR JAVITS: I know, but the government has a hundred billion dollars in FHA upon which it has consistently made money for years and years. That is all the governor is saying. Of course, the government takes only prudent guarantees, but the fact is that guarantees have not been an imposition on the federal budget and, indeed, the government has made a profit from them. Now, that does not mean we should be improvident or reckless, but a revenue-producing operation should be a preferred source of financing. That is all.

MR. LAIRD: And I think it would only be fair to state that if the cities, the counties, and the states want to go into a guarantee program in the future, they will have to be willing to give up something.

GOVERNOR CAREY: Agreed. Agreed.

MR. LAIRD: They will have to give up tax exemptions, and they will have to give up some other things. They will have to pay a premium for their money.

GOVERNOR CAREY: Right.

MR. LAIRD: And it will raise the costs of local and state government. It will not be a freebee for anyone.

Ladies and gentlemen, our time has run out. The American Enterprise Institute has been delighted to present this panel discussion on the financial crisis of our cities, featuring Governor Hugh Carey, Senator Jacob Javits, Senator Charles Percy, and the assistant secretary of the treasury for economic policy, the Honorable Sidney Jones. Mr. Jones represented Secretary Simon on this program today because of the cabinet meeting called by President Ford. We very much appreciate their participation in this program.

Design: Pat Taylor